Cahokia:
The Rise and Fall of an
Ancient American City

Preface

Welcome to this comprehensive book on Cahokia, an ancient city of great significance in North American history. In the following pages, we invite you to embark on a journey of discovery, delving into the fascinating world of Cahokia and exploring its cultural, social, and historical dimensions.

Cahokia, located in what is now the state of Illinois, was once the heart of a thriving pre-Columbian Native American civilization known as the Mississippian culture. This remarkable city flourished between the 9th and 14th centuries, leaving behind a legacy that continues to captivate archaeologists, historians, and enthusiasts to this day.

In this book, we aim to provide a comprehensive overview of Cahokia, drawing upon the latest research and scholarly insights. We will explore various aspects of this ancient city, including its cultural practices, social organization, religious beliefs, trade networks, and political structures. Through our exploration, we hope to unravel the mysteries surrounding Cahokia and shed light on its significance in the broader context of Native American history and archaeology.

Each chapter will delve into a specific theme, allowing us to examine Cahokia from multiple angles and provide a holistic understanding of this ancient civilization. We will explore the layout and architecture of the city, the daily life of its inhabitants, the economic activities and trade networks that contributed to its prosperity, the religious beliefs and ceremonial practices that shaped its spiritual life, and the social and political structures that governed its society.

Furthermore, we will examine the decline of Cahokia and its lasting legacy, as well as the ongoing efforts in excavation, preservation, and research that continue to deepen our understanding of this ancient city.

Throughout this book, we aim to present a balanced and comprehensive account of Cahokia, drawing upon archaeological evidence, historical records, and interdisciplinary research. We recognize the importance of honoring and respecting the perspectives and knowledge of Indigenous communities whose ancestors once inhabited Cahokia's lands.

As you delve into the chapters that follow, we hope you will develop a deeper appreciation for the cultural achievements of Cahokia and its enduring contributions to the tapestry of Native American civilizations. Our journey through time and space will illuminate the complexity, resilience, and rich cultural heritage of the Americas.

We invite you to join us on this captivating exploration of Cahokia, where history, archaeology, and culture converge to reveal the splendor and significance of this ancient city.

T. R. Waven

Table of Contents

Chapter 1

1.1 Introduction

Cahokia, the ancient American city situated across the Mississippi River from present-day St. Louis, Missouri, holds great significance in North American history. Its remarkable size, complexity, and cultural achievements make it a focal point for studying pre-Columbian Native American civilizations. This chapter provides a brief overview of the significance of Cahokia and highlights why studying this ancient city is crucial for our understanding of the indigenous cultures that thrived in the region before European contact.

1.2 The Significance of Cahokia

Cahokia was the largest and most influential urban center of the Mississippian culture, which emerged around 900 CE and persisted until 1500 CE. The Mississippian culture encompassed a vast area, stretching from the Gulf Coast to the Great Lakes, with Cahokia at its heart. The city itself covered approximately six square miles at its peak, boasting a population estimated between 10,000 to 20,000 individuals. These staggering numbers and the urban complexity of Cahokia make it one of the most remarkable archaeological sites in North America.

1.3 Understanding Pre-Columbian Native American Civilizations

The study of Cahokia is instrumental in unraveling the mysteries of pre-Columbian Native American civilizations. Prior to European colonization, a rich tapestry of diverse cultures thrived throughout the Americas, developing unique social, political, economic, and religious systems. However, the historical narratives and perspectives on Native American civilizations have often been overshadowed by the dominant Eurocentric narratives. Exploring Cahokia allows us to challenge and expand our understanding of these civilizations, recognizing their complexity, achievements, and contributions.

1.4 Architectural and Engineering Marvels

Cahokia's architectural and engineering feats are a testament to the sophistication and ingenuity of the Mississippian culture. The city's most striking feature is Monk's Mound, an enormous earthen structure standing over 100 feet tall and covering more than 14 acres. The mounds served as platforms for important buildings, ceremonial spaces, and burial sites. The precise planning, construction techniques, and monumental scale of these mounds demonstrate advanced engineering and organizational capabilities.

1.5 Complex Sociopolitical Organization

Cahokia's social structure and political organization were characterized by hierarchical divisions and a stratified society. Elite ruling classes governed the city, while commoners engaged in various occupations such as farming, craft production, and trade. The political system of Cahokia involved intricate networks of power, diplomacy, and decision-making. By studying the organization and dynamics of Cahokia's society, we gain insights into the complex sociopolitical structures of pre-Columbian Native American cultures.

1.6 Trade, Commerce, and Cultural Exchange

Cahokia served as a hub of regional trade and cultural exchange. Its strategic location near major river systems facilitated trade networks that extended across vast distances. Archaeological evidence reveals a wide array of exotic materials, such as marine shells, copper, flint, and pottery, indicating long-distance trade relationships. Understanding the economic systems and cultural interactions at Cahokia provides valuable insights into the networks of exchange and the economic vitality of ancient Native American societies.

1.7 Environmental Adaptation and Sustainability

Studying Cahokia allows us to examine how ancient societies adapted to and modified their environment for sustenance and survival. The construction of monumental earthen mounds, the cultivation of crops, and the management of resources all required a deep understanding of the local ecology. Investigating the strategies employed by the Cahokian people sheds light on their relationship with the natural world and provides lessons in sustainable practices.

Conclusion:

The significance of Cahokia cannot be overstated in our quest to understand pre-Columbian Native American civilizations

Chapter 2: The Mississippian Culture

2.1 Overview of the Mississippian Culture

The Mississippian culture emerged around 900 CE and flourished until approximately 1500 CE. It encompassed a vast region that stretched from the Gulf Coast to the Great Lakes and from the Appalachian Mountains to the Great Plains. The Mississippian culture is known for its advanced agricultural practices, monumental architecture, complex social organization, and vibrant artistic expressions.

2.2 Cultural Practices

2.2.1 Agriculture and Subsistence

The Mississippian people were skilled farmers who cultivated maize (corn), beans, and squash, commonly known as the "Three Sisters." These crops formed the basis of their diet and allowed for the development of sedentary communities. The cultivation of these crops was accompanied by the construction of terraced fields and the use of advanced agricultural techniques.

2.2.2 Art and Craftsmanship

The Mississippian culture exhibited a rich artistic tradition. Skilled artisans created intricate pottery, often adorned with elaborate designs and motifs. Shell and copper work were also prominent, showcasing the craftsmanship and artistic expression of the culture. These artistic endeavors reflected the cultural values, religious beliefs, and social significance within Mississippian society.

2.2.3 Ceremonialism and Rituals

Ceremonialism played a crucial role in the Mississippian culture. Rituals and religious ceremonies were conducted in large, open plazas, and central gathering places. These ceremonies were likely associated with the religious beliefs and cosmology of the Mississippian people, reinforcing social cohesion and spiritual connections.

2.3 Social Organization

2.3.1 Chiefdoms and Political Structure

The Mississippian culture was organized into hierarchical chiefdoms. Political power was concentrated in the hands of chiefs and ruling elites who exercised authority over various communities. Chiefs played vital roles in the social, political, and religious life of their respective chiefdoms.

2.3.2 Social Stratification

Mississippian societies were stratified, with clear social divisions. The ruling elites held elevated positions in society, often residing in prestigious residences atop the large mounds. Commoners, who comprised the majority of the population, engaged in subsistence agriculture, crafts, and other occupations. This social stratification was reflected in the distribution of wealth, access to resources, and ceremonial roles.

2.4 Religious Beliefs

2.4.1 Cosmology and Spirituality

The Mississippian people held a complex belief system that integrated spiritual beliefs with the natural world. Their cosmology encompassed various deities and supernatural beings associated with natural elements, celestial bodies, and animal spirits. The religious practices and rituals aimed to maintain harmony with the spiritual realm and ensure the well-being of the community.

2.4.2 Symbolism and Sacred Spaces

Sacred spaces and symbolic representations were integral to Mississippian religious practices. Mounds, plazas, and other architectural features held spiritual significance. Mounds, such as the monumental Monk's Mound at Cahokia, served as platforms for important structures and were often associated with religious ceremonies, burial sites, and the dwelling places of powerful individuals.

2.5 Connection between Cahokia and the Broader Mississippian Culture

Cahokia served as the epicenter of the Mississippian culture, exerting significant influence over the surrounding regions. The connections between Cahokia and other Mississippian sites were evident through trade networks, cultural exchanges, and shared religious practices. The distribution of artifacts, architectural similarities, and the presence of distinctive Mississippian traits in multiple locations illustrate the cohesive nature of the Mississippian culture and the interconnectivity among its various settlements.

Conclusion:

The Mississippian culture was a complex and vibrant civilization that left an indelible mark on North American history. Through their advanced agricultural practices, impressive architecture, social organization, and religious beliefs, the Mississippian people created a unique cultural legacy. Cahokia, as the largest and most influential center of the Mississippian culture, played a pivotal role in shaping and disseminating the cultural practices and social dynamics of this fascinating ancient civilization.

Chapter 3: The City of Cahokia

3.1 Location, Geography, and Natural Resources of Cahokia:

Cahokia was situated in the American Bottom region, located across the Mississippi River from present-day St. Louis, Missouri. This location provided access to abundant natural resources and a fertile environment suitable for agriculture. The American Bottom was characterized by rich alluvial soils, forests, and proximity to waterways, making it an ideal location for the establishment of a thriving city.

3.2 Layout and Architecture of the City

3.2.1 Mound Complexes

Cahokia was distinguished by its impressive earthen mounds, which played a central role in the city's layout and architecture. The most prominent of these mounds was Monk's Mound, a massive earthen structure covering over 14 acres and standing more than 100 feet tall. Other mounds within Cahokia included Rattlesnake Mound, Twin Mounds, and the Mound of the Twin Warriors. These mounds served multiple purposes, including platforms for important buildings, burial sites, and markers of ceremonial and political significance.

3.2.2 Central Plaza

The central plaza of Cahokia, known as the Grand Plaza, was a focal point of the city's social and ceremonial activities. This large open space, surrounded by mounds and elite residences, served as a gathering place for communal events, rituals, and public gatherings.

The plaza was a hub of social interaction, trade, and religious ceremonies, reflecting the importance of community and cultural exchange within Cahokia.

3.2.3 Palisade and Defensive Structures

Cahokia was protected by a wooden palisade, a defensive wall made of vertically positioned logs. This palisade enclosed a significant portion of the city and provided a level of security for its inhabitants. Additionally, guard towers were strategically positioned along the palisade, enhancing the defensive capabilities of the city.

3.3 Population Estimates and Daily Life in Cahokia

3.3.1 Population Estimates

The population of Cahokia at its peak is estimated to have been between 10,000 and 20,000 individuals. This significant population made Cahokia one of the largest urban centers in pre-Columbian North America. The diverse population consisted of ruling elites, commoners, artisans, farmers, traders, and religious specialists.

3.3.2 Residential Areas

Cahokia encompassed various residential areas where people lived and carried out their daily activities. The elite ruling class resided in grand residences atop the mounds, showcasing their status and authority. Commoners inhabited smaller houses made of wattle and daub, which were rectangular in shape and often organized around central courtyards. These houses formed compact neighborhoods within the city, fostering social cohesion and community interaction.

3.3.3 Subsistence and Economy

The economy of Cahokia was primarily based on agriculture. The Mississippian people cultivated maize, beans, squash, and other crops to sustain the population. Cahokia's strategic location near rivers and trade routes facilitated economic exchanges, making it a hub for regional trade. Traders brought a variety of goods, including raw materials, exotic items, and craft products, contributing to the economic vitality of the city.

3.3.4 Social and Cultural Life

Daily life in Cahokia involved a range of activities, including farming, craft production, religious ceremonies, and communal gatherings. The city's social structure was hierarchical, with the ruling elite exerting influence over political, economic, and religious affairs. Religion played a significant role in the lives of the Cahokian people, and religious ceremonies and rituals were conducted in the central plaza and on the mounds.

Conclusion:

Cahokia's strategic location, impressive architectural features, and significant population made it a thriving urban center of the Mississippian culture. The layout and design of the city, characterized by monumental mounds, a central plaza, and residential areas, reflected the social, political, and cultural dynamics of its inhabitants.

Understanding the geography, architecture, and daily life in Cahokia provides valuable insights into the complexity and achievements of this ancient American city.

Chapter 4: Trade and Economy

4.1 Importance of Trade Networks and Commerce in Cahokia's Prosperity

Trade and commerce played a vital role in the prosperity and growth of Cahokia. The city's strategic location near major river systems, including the Mississippi and Illinois Rivers, positioned it as a central hub for regional trade networks. The exchange of goods and resources not only contributed to the economic vitality of Cahokia but also fostered cultural interaction, social ties, and the dissemination of ideas and innovations.

4.2 Description of Trade Routes, Goods Exchanged, and Economic Activities

4.2.1 Trade Routes

Cahokia's trade routes extended across vast distances, connecting the city to various regions and cultures. The Mississippi and Illinois Rivers served as important transportation corridors, facilitating the movement of goods and people. Overland routes, including trails and footpaths, linked Cahokia to neighboring communities and distant trade partners. These trade routes formed the lifelines of commerce, ensuring the flow of goods and ideas into and out of Cahokia.

4.2.2 Goods Exchanged

A wide array of goods was exchanged through Cahokia's trade networks. Locally produced items, such as agricultural products (maize, beans, squash), pottery, flint, and woodcraft, were traded within the region. Exotic goods from distant areas, including marine shells, copper, mica, obsidian, and ceremonial objects, also found their way to Cahokia. These materials represented both utilitarian and symbolic value, enhancing the prestige and wealth of the city.

4.2.3 Economic Activities

Economic activities in Cahokia encompassed various occupations and specialized crafts. Agriculture formed the backbone of the economy, with the cultivation of crops providing sustenance for the population. Craftsmanship thrived, with artisans producing pottery, shell ornaments, copper objects, textiles, and other goods. Cahokia's skilled craftsmen played a crucial role in the production of items for both local consumption and trade. Additionally, trade itself became a significant economic activity, with traders facilitating the exchange of goods and facilitating regional commerce.

4.3 Role of Cahokia as a Regional Trade Hub and Its Connections to Other Native American Societies

4.3.1 Regional Trade Hub

Cahokia's central position within the Mississippian culture made it a key regional trade hub. Goods from various communities and regions converged in Cahokia, creating a vibrant marketplace where exchange and commerce thrived. The city's economic prosperity relied on its ability to facilitate trade and maintain strong connections with neighboring communities.

4.3.2 Connections to Other Native American Societies

Cahokia's trade networks extended beyond its immediate surroundings, connecting it to other Native American societies. Through these trade connections, Cahokia established economic, social, and cultural ties with distant communities. Exchanges with societies such as the Caddo, the Hopewell, and the Southeastern tribes facilitated the flow of goods, ideas, and cultural practices. These connections fostered interregional trade networks, enhanced diplomatic relationships, and contributed to the cultural diversity and richness of Cahokia.

4.3.3 Cultural Interaction and Exchange

Trade not only facilitated economic transactions but also enabled cultural interaction and the exchange of ideas. Through commerce, Cahokia became a melting pot of diverse cultures, with individuals from different regions coming together to engage in trade and share their knowledge and beliefs. This cultural exchange contributed to the development of a vibrant and dynamic society within Cahokia, fostering innovation, artistic expressions, and the transmission of cultural practices.

Conclusion:

Trade and commerce were integral to the prosperity and growth of Cahokia. The city's central location, well-established trade networks, and diverse range of exchanged goods allowed it to thrive as a regional trade hub. Through these trade connections, Cahokia formed strong economic, social, and cultural ties with neighboring communities, contributing to its significance as a vibrant and interconnected center of pre-Columbian Native American civilization.

Chapter 5: Social and Political Structure

5.1 Hierarchical Social Structure and Class Divisions in Cahokia

Cahokia had a hierarchical social structure characterized by distinct class divisions. This social hierarchy determined individuals' roles, access to resources, and levels of prestige within the community.

5.1.1 Ruling Elite

At the top of the social structure were the ruling elites, who held positions of power and authority. These elites comprised the political and religious leaders of Cahokia, including chiefs and high-ranking officials. They resided in prestigious residences atop the mounds and controlled the allocation of resources, oversaw religious ceremonies, and made decisions that affected the community as a whole. The ruling elite enjoyed privileges, such as access to luxury goods, ceremonial regalia, and specialized knowledge.

5.1.2 Commoners

Beneath the ruling elite were the commoners, who constituted the majority of the population. Commoners engaged in various occupations such as farming, craft production, and trade. They lived in smaller houses within residential areas and contributed to the economic and social fabric of Cahokia. While commoners had less political influence and access to resources compared to the ruling elite, they played important roles in sustaining the city's economy and community life.

5.2 Roles and Responsibilities of the Ruling Elite and Commoners

5.2.1 Ruling Elite

The ruling elite in Cahokia held significant responsibilities and duties within the community. They provided leadership, maintained social order, and acted as intermediaries between the human realm and the spiritual realm. Ruling elites were responsible for making political decisions, overseeing the allocation of resources, conducting religious ceremonies, and upholding the well-being and prosperity of the city. Their positions of authority bestowed them with considerable influence and prestige.

5.2.2 Commoners

Commoners in Cahokia played essential roles in sustaining the city's economy and daily life. They were primarily engaged in agricultural activities, tending to fields, and ensuring food production for the community. Commoners also participated in craft production, creating pottery, textiles, and other goods that contributed to local consumption and trade. Additionally, they took part in trade networks, both as producers and consumers. Commoners contributed to the cultural and social fabric of Cahokia through their participation in communal events, religious ceremonies, and the maintenance of daily life within the city.

5.3 Political Organization and Governance in Cahokia

5.3.1 Chiefdoms

Cahokia's political organization was structured around chiefdoms, which were led by chiefs and ruling elites. Chiefdoms represented social and political units that encompassed multiple communities and settlements. Chiefs held authority over their respective chiefdoms, making decisions regarding resource allocation, trade, defense, and ceremonial activities. Chiefdoms within Cahokia's sphere of influence may have had varying degrees of autonomy but likely maintained connections with the central authority in Cahokia.

5.3.2 Political Power and Decision-making

Political power in Cahokia was concentrated in the hands of the ruling elite, particularly the chiefs. The chiefs held authority based on their lineage, charisma, military prowess, and ability to maintain the support of their communities. They made decisions in consultation with other elites and held considerable influence over the social, economic, and religious aspects of Cahokia. The governance structure in Cahokia allowed for both centralized decision-making and regional autonomy within chiefdoms.

5.3.3 Social Cohesion and Control

Political organization and governance in Cahokia played a crucial role in maintaining social cohesion and control within the city. The ruling elite, through their authority and decision-making, ensured the well-being and stability of the community. They fostered social cohesion through religious rituals, communal gatherings, and the redistribution of resources. The political organization of Cahokia contributed to the overall functioning of the city and the preservation of its social order.

Conclusion:

Cahokia's social and political structure was characterized by hierarchical divisions and a clear distinction between the ruling elite and commoners. The ruling elite held positions of power, overseeing governance, religious practices, and resource allocation. Commoners formed the majority of the population and played vital roles in sustaining the city's economy and daily life. The political organization of Cahokia revolved around chiefdoms, with chiefs serving as central figures of authority. The social and political structure of Cahokia facilitated social cohesion, maintained order, and contributed to the city's cultural and political dynamics.

Chapter 6: Religion and Ceremonial Life

6.1 Spiritual Beliefs and Religious Practices of the Cahokian People

The Cahokian people had a rich spiritual belief system that played a central role in their lives. Their religious practices encompassed a complex set of beliefs, rituals, and ceremonies that connected them with the spiritual realm and the natural world.

6.1.1 Cosmology and Beliefs

Cahokians believed in a complex cosmology that emphasized the interconnections between humans, nature, and the spiritual realm. They believed in the presence of powerful spiritual beings and deities associated with natural forces such as the sun, moon, rivers, and fertility. These spiritual entities played a significant role in their daily lives and were believed to influence the well-being and prosperity of the community.

6.1.2 Ancestor Worship

Ancestor worship was a prominent aspect of Cahokian religious practices. Ancestors were venerated and considered intermediaries between the living and the spiritual realm. The Cahokian people believed that the spirits of their ancestors guided and protected them, and they conducted rituals and ceremonies to honor and seek their blessings.

6.1.3 Shamanism and Ritual Specialists

Shamans and ritual specialists held important roles in Cahokian religious practices. They acted as intermediaries between the human and spiritual realms, conducting rituals, performing healing practices, and communicating with spiritual entities. These individuals possessed specialized knowledge, skills, and abilities, and played a crucial role in maintaining the spiritual well-being of the community.

6.2 Description of Major Religious Sites and Rituals

6.2.1 Sacred Mounds

The monumental earthen mounds of Cahokia served as significant religious sites. These mounds were believed to be sacred places where rituals, ceremonies, and offerings to the spiritual beings were conducted. The largest mound, Monk's Mound, likely held particular religious and ceremonial importance, symbolizing the connection between the earthly and spiritual realms.

6.2.2 Central Plaza and Ceremonial Gatherings

The central plaza of Cahokia served as a focal point for communal gatherings and religious ceremonies. It was a space where the community came together to participate in rituals, dances, feasts, and other ceremonial activities. The central plaza played a crucial role in fostering social cohesion, religious expression, and the strengthening of community bonds.

6.2.3 Burial Mounds

Burial mounds were also significant religious sites in Cahokia. These mounds served as resting places for the deceased and were believed to be sacred spaces where the spirits of the ancestors resided. Ceremonies and rituals were conducted at these burial mounds to honor the ancestors and ensure their continued protection and guidance.

6.3 Relationship between Religion, Power, and Social Cohesion in Cahokia

6.3.1 Religious Legitimization of Power

Religion played a crucial role in legitimizing the power of the ruling elite in Cahokia. The ruling elite, including chiefs and religious leaders, utilized religious beliefs and rituals to reinforce their authority and establish a connection with the spiritual realm. They claimed a special relationship with the spiritual entities, positioning themselves as mediators between the divine and the human, thereby strengthening their political and social position.

6.3.2 Social Cohesion and Community Identity

Religion and ceremonial life in Cahokia were central to fostering social cohesion and maintaining a sense of community identity. Religious rituals and communal gatherings brought people together, reinforcing shared beliefs, values, and practices. These ceremonies provided a sense of belonging and collective purpose, enhancing social cohesion and unity within the community.

6.3.3 Role of Religion in Daily Life

Religion permeated various aspects of daily life in Cahokia. It influenced agricultural practices, guiding planting and harvest rituals to ensure bountiful crops. Religious beliefs and rituals also shaped social norms, ethical codes, and moral values within the community. The presence of religion in daily life fostered a sense of spiritual interconnectedness, providing individuals with a framework for understanding the world around them.

Conclusion:

Religion and ceremonial life held immense significance in Cahokia. The Cahokian people's spiritual beliefs and practices were deeply intertwined with their social, cultural, and political systems. Religious rituals, sacred sites, and beliefs served to establish a connection with the spiritual realm, reinforce power structures, foster social cohesion, and provide individuals with a sense of identity and purpose within the community. Understanding the role of religion in Cahokia allows us to appreciate the profound impact it had on the lives and worldview of its inhabitants.

Chapter 7: Decline and Legacy

7.1 Theories and Debates Surrounding the Decline of Cahokia

The decline of Cahokia remains a topic of scholarly debate, with various theories proposed to explain the city's decline. While the exact reasons are still uncertain, several factors have been suggested as potential contributors to the decline of Cahokia.

7.1.1 Environmental Changes

One theory suggests that environmental changes played a significant role in the decline of Cahokia. This includes factors such as soil depletion, deforestation, and the impact of climatic shifts. Over time, extensive agricultural practices and the demand for wood resources may have led to soil erosion and reduced agricultural productivity. Droughts, floods, or other environmental disruptions could have further strained the city's resources and contributed to its decline.

7.1.2 Sociopolitical Unrest

Another theory focuses on internal sociopolitical factors as a cause of decline. It suggests that conflicts, social unrest, or political instability within Cahokia may have weakened the city's centralized power structures. Disputes over resources, changing power dynamics, or a breakdown in social cohesion could have led to internal divisions, weakening the city's ability to sustain itself and maintain its influence.

7.1.3 External Factors and Invasion

Some theories propose that external factors, such as conflicts with neighboring societies or the arrival of new populations, contributed to the decline of Cahokia. Increased competition for resources, warfare, or the displacement of populations might have disrupted the social and economic stability of the city, leading to its eventual decline.

7.2 Possible Factors Contributing to the City's Decline

7.2.1 Environmental Changes

Cahokia's reliance on intensive agriculture and deforestation may have led to ecological degradation and reduced agricultural productivity over time. Soil depletion, erosion, and the loss of forest resources could have strained the city's ability to sustain its population and maintain its economic and social structures.

7.2.2 Sociopolitical Factors

Internal conflicts, social unrest, or political instability within Cahokia may have contributed to its decline. Changing power dynamics, factionalism, or the breakdown of social cohesion could have weakened the city's ability to govern effectively and maintain its centralized authority.

7.2.3 Epidemics and Disease

The introduction of new diseases by contact with European explorers and settlers is also considered a potential factor in the decline of Cahokia. The spread of infectious diseases, to which the Cahokian population may have had little resistance, could have caused significant mortality, leading to population decline and social disruption.

7.3 Influence and Legacy of Cahokia on Later Native American Cultures and Modern Society

7.3.1 Cultural Influence

Cahokia's influence extended beyond its own time and place, shaping the development of later Native American cultures. The architectural and artistic styles, religious beliefs, and social practices that originated in Cahokia reverberated throughout the region, influencing subsequent Native American societies. Elements of Cahokian culture can be seen in the artistic traditions, mound-building practices, and religious beliefs of later Native American civilizations.

7.3.2 Mound-Building Tradition

The legacy of Cahokia is most evident in its monumental earthen mounds. The mound-building tradition established by Cahokia spread across the Mississippi River Valley and influenced the construction of mounds by subsequent Native American cultures. Mound sites such as Etowah in Georgia, Moundville in Alabama, and Spiro in Oklahoma exhibit architectural similarities to Cahokia, indicating a cultural and architectural continuity.

7.3.3 Cultural Memory and Heritage

The legacy of Cahokia continues to hold significance in modern society. The archaeological remains and cultural heritage associated with

Cahokia are preserved and studied, providing insights into the history, achievements, and complexities of pre-Columbian Native American civilizations. Cahokia serves as a reminder of the sophisticated and organized societies that existed prior to European contact, challenging conventional narratives about the complexity of Native American civilizations.

7.3.4 Tourist Attraction and Education

Cahokia's monumental mounds and archaeological site attract visitors from around the world, serving as an educational and cultural tourism destination. The site provides an opportunity for the public to learn about the history and cultural heritage of the Cahokian people and promotes a better understanding of the diversity and richness of Native American civilizations.

Conclusion:

The decline of Cahokia remains a topic of debate, with environmental changes and sociopolitical factors suggested as possible causes. Despite its decline, Cahokia's influence and legacy are profound. Its cultural, architectural, and religious practices influenced later Native American cultures, and its mound-building tradition left an indelible mark on the landscape of the Mississippi River Valley. The preservation and study of Cahokia's remains contribute to our understanding of pre-Columbian Native American civilizations and challenge our perceptions of the complexity and sophistication of indigenous societies.

Chapter 8: Excavations and Preservation

8.1 Overview of Archaeological Excavations and Discoveries at Cahokia

Archaeological excavations at Cahokia have played a pivotal role in uncovering the history, architecture, and cultural practices of the ancient city. Excavations have provided valuable insights into the lives of the Cahokian people, their social structure, religious beliefs, and economic activities.

8.1.1 Early Excavations

The first systematic excavations at Cahokia began in the late 19th century, with notable archaeologists such as Warren K. Moorehead and Melvin Fowler leading the efforts. These early excavations focused primarily on uncovering the monumental mounds and their contents. Excavations revealed elaborate burial practices, ceremonial objects, pottery, tools, and evidence of daily life in Cahokia.

8.1.2 Advanced Techniques and Modern Excavations

In recent decades, advances in archaeological techniques and methodologies have allowed for more comprehensive and nuanced excavations at Cahokia. The use of ground-penetrating radar, aerial surveys, and non-invasive techniques has aided in mapping the site's extent and identifying structures hidden beneath the surface. These modern excavations have uncovered additional mounds, residential areas, workshops, and evidence of complex urban planning.

8.1.3 Discoveries and Findings

Excavations at Cahokia have yielded a wealth of archaeological findings. These include artifacts such as pottery, stone tools, shell ornaments, copper jewelry, and ceremonial objects. The discovery of the Woodhenge sun calendar, a large circular structure used for astronomical observations and tracking the seasons, provided valuable insights into the Cahokian people's knowledge of celestial events. Burial mounds have revealed information about burial practices, social status, and the presence of grave goods, shedding light on the beliefs and customs of the Cahokian society.

8.2 Discussion of Preservation Efforts and the Establishment of Cahokia Mounds State Historic Site

Recognizing the cultural and historical significance of Cahokia, preservation efforts have been undertaken to protect and conserve the archaeological remains of the ancient city.

8.2.1 Establishment of Cahokia Mounds State Historic Site

In 1929, the state of Illinois established Cahokia Mounds State Historic Site, encompassing a significant portion of the Cahokia archaeological complex. The site comprises over 2,200 acres and includes several mounds, plazas, and interpretive centers. The establishment of the historic site ensures the preservation of the mounds and provides a platform for education and public engagement.

8.2.2 Conservation and Site Management

Preservation efforts at Cahokia Mounds State Historic Site include conservation practices, maintenance of the mounds and structures, and ongoing research to understand and protect the site's fragile archaeological remains. Archaeologists, historians, and conservators work collaboratively to monitor the site, develop preservation strategies, and educate visitors about the significance of Cahokia.

8.2.3 Interpretation and Visitor Experience

Cahokia Mounds State Historic Site offers interpretive programs, guided tours, and educational exhibits to enhance visitors' understanding of Cahokia's history and cultural heritage. Interpretive centers provide insights into the daily life, religious practices, and social organization of the Cahokian people. These efforts ensure that the site remains accessible to the public while promoting responsible stewardship and appreciation of its significance.

8.3 Importance of Ongoing Research and Future Prospects for Understanding Cahokia

Ongoing research at Cahokia continues to deepen our understanding of the ancient city and its inhabitants. Future prospects for understanding Cahokia are promising, thanks to advancements in technology, interdisciplinary approaches, and collaborative research efforts.

8.3.1 Interdisciplinary Approaches

Interdisciplinary research involving archaeology, anthropology, geology, ecology, and other fields contributes to a comprehensive understanding of Cahokia. These multidisciplinary approaches allow for the integration of various data sources, including material culture, environmental data, and historical records, to reconstruct the social, cultural, and ecological dynamics of the Cahokian society.

8.3.2 Technological Advancements

Advancements in archaeological technologies, such as remote sensing, isotopic analysis, DNA studies, and digital modeling, provide new avenues for investigating Cahokia. These technologies can reveal hidden structures, analyze artifacts with greater precision, and explore ancient DNA to understand population movements and genetic relationships.

8.3.3 Collaborative Research

Collaborative research projects involving academic institutions, Native American tribes, and community organizations are essential for advancing our knowledge of Cahokia. Engaging with descendant communities and integrating indigenous perspectives fosters a more inclusive and nuanced understanding of the history and legacy of Cahokia.

Conclusion:

Excavations at Cahokia have unearthed a wealth of archaeological evidence, providing invaluable insights into the ancient city's history and culture. Preservation efforts, including the establishment of Cahokia Mounds State Historic Site, ensure the protection and accessibility of the site for future generations. Ongoing research, utilizing interdisciplinary approaches and technological advancements, continues to shed light on the complexities of Cahokia and its significance within North American history. The exploration and study of Cahokia's past hold great potential for deepening our understanding of pre-Columbian Native American civilizations and their enduring legacies.

Chapter 9: Art and Symbolism

Artistic expression played a significant role in the culture of Cahokia, offering a window into the aesthetic sensibilities, belief systems, and cultural practices of the ancient city. In this chapter, we will explore the diverse artistic expressions found in Cahokia, including pottery, sculptures, and rock art. We will delve into the meaning and cultural significance of these artistic creations, providing insights into Cahokia's aesthetics and belief systems.

9.1 Pottery

Pottery was a prominent form of artistic expression in Cahokia. The ceramic vessels produced by Cahokian potters showcased their skill and creativity. These vessels varied in shape, size, and decoration, reflecting different functional and ceremonial purposes. Intricate designs, such as geometric patterns, animal motifs, and human figures, adorned the pottery surfaces. These designs were often achieved through techniques such as incising, appliqué, and painting.

The symbolism behind Cahokian pottery remains subject to interpretation. Some designs may have represented clan symbols or spiritual entities, while others might have conveyed cosmological or mythological narratives. The presence of certain motifs, such as the birdman or the spider, suggests a connection to Cahokia's religious and cosmological beliefs. The use of distinctive color combinations, such as red and white, may have carried symbolic meaning related to fertility, life cycles, or spiritual realms.

9.2 Sculptures

Sculptures found at Cahokia offer fascinating insights into the artistic expressions of the ancient city. The most well-known sculptures are the famous "birdman" figurines. These figurines depict a human figure adorned with avian attributes, emphasizing the connection between humans and birds in Cahokian cosmology. The birdman imagery likely held symbolic and ritualistic significance, possibly representing a supernatural or ancestral being.

Other sculptures discovered at Cahokia include figurines of animals, such as bears, falcons, and mythical creatures. These animal representations may have played roles in religious rituals, symbolizing certain powers or embodying specific spiritual forces. The craftsmanship and attention to detail in these sculptures attest to the artistic skill and cultural significance attached to these objects.

9.3 Rock Art

Cahokia also features rock art, although it is relatively rare compared to other forms of artistic expression. Petroglyphs and pictographs can be found on rocks and cliff faces near Cahokia. These rock art sites exhibit various motifs, including animal and human figures, abstract symbols, and geometric patterns. The meanings behind these rock art depictions are not fully understood, but they likely held religious, symbolic, or ceremonial significance.

The study of Cahokia's rock art provides glimpses into the ancient rituals, spiritual beliefs, and cultural practices of the Cahokian people. It offers valuable evidence of their connection with the natural landscape and their desire to leave lasting marks of their presence and beliefs.

9.4 Cultural Significance

The artistic expressions of Cahokia were not merely decorative but held deep cultural and symbolic meanings. They played a vital role in religious ceremonies, rituals, and social gatherings, reflecting the spiritual and cosmological beliefs of the Cahokian people. Art served as a means of communication, storytelling, and expression of identity within the community.

The aesthetics and symbolism in Cahokian art also demonstrate the complex interplay between humans, animals, and the natural world. The birdman imagery, for example, suggests a belief in the interdependence and interconnectedness of humans and avian creatures, reflecting a worldview that acknowledged the significance of the natural environment.

Through the analysis of artistic creations in Cahokia, researchers gain insights into the aesthetic preferences, mythologies, and spiritual practices of the ancient city's inhabitants. The study of Cahokian art enhances our understanding of the cultural, social, and religious dimensions of Cahokia, helping to reconstruct the rich tapestry of its past.

Conclusion:

The artistic expressions found in Cahokia, including pottery, sculptures, and rock art, are not only visually captivating but also offer profound insights into the beliefs, values, and cosmology of the ancient city. The elaborate designs and symbolic motifs found in Cahokian art reflect the cultural and spiritual significance attached to these creations, revealing a society deeply connected to its natural surroundings and invested in the expression of its cultural identity.

Chapter 10: Astronomy and Cosmology

Cahokia's understanding and observation of celestial phenomena played a significant role in their culture and belief systems. In this chapter, we will delve into the fascinating field of Cahokian astronomy and cosmology. We will investigate their knowledge of the heavens, explore the astronomical alignments and structures within Cahokia, and examine the rituals that reflect the Cahokian people's relationship with the cosmos.

10.1 Celestial Phenomena and Knowledge

The Cahokian people possessed a sophisticated understanding of celestial events and their cyclical nature. Through keen observation of the sky, they tracked the movements of the sun, moon, and stars, identifying patterns and incorporating them into their daily lives, rituals, and agricultural practices. The ability to predict celestial events, such as solstices, equinoxes, and lunar phases, was crucial for determining agricultural calendars and timing significant cultural and religious ceremonies.

The Cahokians recognized the importance of celestial bodies in shaping their worldview and understanding of the cosmos. The sun, with its life-giving warmth and light, held immense significance. The moon, with its rhythmic cycles, guided the Cahokian calendar and marked the passage of time. Stars, constellations, and other celestial bodies were likely incorporated into Cahokian cosmology, reflecting their beliefs about the interconnectedness of the earthly and celestial realms.

10.2 Astronomical Alignments and Structures

Cahokia's built environment exhibits remarkable alignments with celestial phenomena, indicating an intentional incorporation of astronomical knowledge into their architecture and urban planning. The most renowned example is the alignment of Monks Mound, the largest mound at Cahokia, with the sunrise on the spring and fall equinoxes. This alignment suggests a deliberate orientation of the mound to capture the solar phenomena associated with these key points in the astronomical calendar.

Other mounds and structures at Cahokia may have also been aligned with celestial events, although their precise alignments and purposes are still being studied. Researchers have proposed alignments with the solstices, lunar standstills, and other significant celestial moments. These alignments would have allowed the Cahokians to mark and celebrate important astronomical events in their communal spaces.

10.3 Rituals and Cosmological

Connections Astronomy was intertwined with the spiritual and religious beliefs of the Cahokian people. Ceremonies and rituals conducted at Cahokia likely incorporated astronomical events and symbolism, reinforcing their cosmological connections. The alignment of structures with celestial events would have served as a backdrop for these rituals, enhancing their symbolic significance.

The observation and celebration of celestial phenomena may have been integral to Cahokian religious ceremonies. Solstices and equinoxes, for example, mark crucial moments in the solar year and may have been associated with agricultural fertility, renewal, or spiritual transformation. Lunar phases and lunar standstills may have also been linked to specific rites and rituals.

10.4 Legacy and Significance

Cahokia's knowledge of astronomy and its integration into their culture underscores their sophisticated understanding of the cosmos and their desire to establish a harmonious relationship with the celestial realm. The deliberate alignment of structures and incorporation of celestial events into rituals suggest a deep reverence for the natural world and a belief in the interconnectedness of all things.

The study of Cahokian astronomy and cosmology not only sheds light on their scientific and astronomical achievements but also provides insights into their cultural, spiritual, and social dimensions. It emphasizes the importance of celestial phenomena in shaping their worldview and the integral role of the cosmos in their daily lives and belief systems.

Conclusion:

Cahokia's understanding of celestial phenomena, its astronomical alignments, and the incorporation of celestial events into rituals reveal a sophisticated knowledge of the cosmos and a deep spiritual connection with the celestial realm. The study of Cahokian astronomy and cosmology enriches our understanding of their culture, worldview, and their intricate relationship with the natural and celestial worlds.

Chapter 11: Agriculture and Foodways

Agriculture formed the foundation of Cahokia's society, providing sustenance for its population and facilitating the city's growth and development. In this chapter, we will delve into the agricultural practices of Cahokia, exploring crop cultivation, land management strategies, and food production. We will examine the significance of agriculture in sustaining the population and supporting the city's expansion.

11.1 Crop Cultivation

Cahokia's agricultural practices centered around the cultivation of crops that were essential for food production. The primary crops grown by the Cahokian people included maize (corn), beans, and squash, known as the "Three Sisters." This agricultural trio provided a balanced diet, as each crop complemented the others in terms of nutritional value and growing requirements. Maize served as a staple grain, beans enriched the soil with nitrogen, and squash acted as ground cover, suppressing weeds and retaining moisture.

Cahokian farmers employed a variety of techniques to cultivate crops. They practiced a form of agriculture called "intensive gardening," which involved creating raised garden beds or mounds and employing techniques such as intercropping and crop rotation. Intercropping involved planting multiple crops in the same field, maximizing space utilization and promoting mutual benefits between the plants. Crop rotation helped maintain soil fertility by alternating crops in specific cycles, reducing the depletion of nutrients.

11.2 Land Management

Cahokia's agricultural success relied on effective land management strategies. The Cahokian people utilized a combination of agricultural techniques to maximize productivity and minimize environmental impact. They engaged in extensive land clearance, removing trees and undergrowth to create arable fields. Controlled burns were also used to clear vegetation and replenish the soil with nutrients, allowing for more productive agricultural practices.

To address potential challenges of flooding, Cahokian farmers implemented techniques such as building elevated garden beds and terraces. These adaptations allowed them to make productive use of floodplain areas and effectively manage water resources. By developing effective land management practices, the Cahokians were able to expand their agricultural activities and support a growing population.

11.3 Food Production and Distribution

Food production in Cahokia was a communal effort, with specialized individuals involved in various stages of the process. Farmers worked the fields, cultivating and harvesting crops, while others were engaged in food processing and storage. The surplus agricultural produce was stored in underground storage pits or granaries, ensuring a stable food supply throughout the year. This surplus facilitated trade and exchange with neighboring communities, contributing to the city's economic prosperity.

The distribution of food within Cahokia was likely organized through a system of communal sharing and social networks. Food would have been distributed to individuals and families based on social and cultural norms, ensuring equitable access to resources within the community. Additionally, the surplus food produced in Cahokia played a crucial role in supporting the city's population and attracting migrants from surrounding regions.

11.4 Significance of Agriculture

Agriculture was fundamental to the success and growth of Cahokia. The adoption of intensive gardening techniques and effective land management strategies enabled the Cahokian people to sustain a large population and support the development of a complex urban center. The surplus food production facilitated social and economic stability, allowing for specialized occupations, trade networks, and the concentration of political and religious power within the city.

Furthermore, agriculture played a significant role in shaping the cultural and social fabric of Cahokia. It fostered a sense of communal identity, as individuals worked collectively towards the shared goal of food production and security. Agricultural rituals and ceremonies likely held spiritual and symbolic significance, reinforcing the importance of agriculture in Cahokian cosmology and belief systems.

Conclusion:

Cahokia's agricultural practices were central to its societal development and growth. Through sophisticated crop cultivation techniques, land management strategies, and communal food production, the Cahokian people not only sustained themselves but also established a thriving urban center. Agriculture served as the backbone of their civilization, contributing to social cohesion, economic prosperity, and cultural identity.

Chapter 12: Gender and Society

Gender roles, relationships, and power dynamics played a significant role in shaping the social fabric of Cahokia. In this chapter, we will delve into the complex dynamics of gender in Cahokia society, exploring the roles of women and men in different spheres of life, including economic activities, religious practices, and political structures. We will analyze the gendered division of labor, the influence of gender on social hierarchies, and the ways in which gender intersected with other aspects of identity in Cahokian society.

12.1 Gendered Division of Labor

In Cahokia, gender influenced the division of labor, with men and women undertaking distinct roles and responsibilities. Women primarily engaged in agricultural activities, including planting, harvesting, and processing crops. Their expertise in horticulture, particularly in cultivating the "Three Sisters" (maize, beans, and squash), was crucial for food production and sustenance. Women also played a significant role in craft production, such as pottery making and textile weaving.

Men, on the other hand, were often involved in hunting, fishing, and clearing land for agriculture. They also participated in trade and warfare, activities that brought prestige and contributed to their social status. The division of labor, while emphasizing different spheres of activity for men and women, was interconnected and mutually supportive, highlighting the interdependence between genders within Cahokian society.

12.2 Power and Social Hierarchies

Power dynamics within Cahokia society were influenced by gender, among other factors. While men generally held positions of political leadership and authority, women also wielded influence and occupied significant roles within their communities. Matrilineal descent and kinship systems likely played a role in shaping social structures, with female lineages potentially transmitting positions of power and authority.

Religious roles and ceremonies provided additional avenues for women to exercise influence. Some archaeological evidence suggests the presence of female religious leaders or priestesses, indicating the recognition of women's spiritual power and their involvement in guiding religious practices. Women may have held esteemed positions within religious hierarchies, contributing to the social and spiritual cohesion of Cahokian society.

12.3 Gender and Rituals

Religious and ceremonial life in Cahokia intersected with gender roles and practices. Rituals and ceremonies often involved both men and women, with each gender contributing unique perspectives and roles.

Gender-specific rituals and ceremonies may have taken place, reinforcing social and spiritual connections.

The Mississippian culture, of which Cahokia was a part, placed significant emphasis on fertility and the life-giving powers of women. Some ceremonies likely centered around women's roles in fertility, childbirth, and the nurturing of life. These rituals not only reinforced gender roles but also emphasized the vital contributions of women to the continuity and prosperity of Cahokian society.

12.4 Gender and Social Identity

Gender intersected with other aspects of identity, such as age, social class, and kinship ties, in shaping individual and collective identities in Cahokia. Social status and prestige were not solely determined by gender but were influenced by factors such as lineage, occupation, and religious affiliations.

While men may have held positions of political leadership, women's roles as mothers, clan leaders, and custodians of cultural knowledge were highly valued. Gender, in conjunction with other social identities, contributed to the overall social complexity and diversity within Cahokia, highlighting the multidimensional nature of identity and power dynamics in pre-Columbian Native American societies.

Conclusion:

Gender roles, relationships, and power dynamics were integral components of Cahokia society. The gendered division of labor, the influence of gender on social hierarchies, and the intersection of gender with religious and ceremonial practices all shaped the social fabric of Cahokia. Understanding the complexities of gender in Cahokian society enhances our appreciation of the diverse roles and contributions of women and men, and provides insights into the complexities of gender dynamics in pre-Columbian Native American civilizations.

Chapter 13: Conflict and Warfare

Conflict and warfare were inherent aspects of Cahokia's complex social and political landscape. In this chapter, we will explore the practices of warfare, intergroup conflicts, and territorial disputes within the Cahokian context. By analyzing archaeological evidence and historical accounts, we can gain insights into the nature of warfare in Cahokia and its impact on the society.

13.1 Warfare Practices

Warfare in Cahokia encompassed a range of activities, including intergroup conflicts, raids, and defensive strategies. The Mississippian culture, of which Cahokia was a part, saw the emergence of fortified settlements and defensive structures, suggesting the need for protection and defense against external threats. Palisades, earthen embankments, and moats surrounded some Cahokian settlements, serving as deterrents and fortifications.

Archaeological evidence, such as the presence of fortifications and defensive palisades, suggests the strategic planning and preparedness of Cahokian communities in times of conflict. The Cahokian people may have employed a variety of weapons, including bows and arrows, spears, and stone-bladed knives, for both offensive and defensive purposes.

13.2 Intergroup Conflicts

Cahokia's political and economic influence extended beyond its immediate vicinity, resulting in interactions, alliances, and conflicts with neighboring communities. Archaeological evidence points to intergroup conflicts and territorial disputes, likely driven by competition for resources, political control, and social prestige. Defensive structures, such as palisades and fortified mounds, suggest that conflicts were not uncommon, and communities were prepared to defend their interests.

Historical accounts from European explorers and early settlers also provide insights into intergroup conflicts in the region. Descriptions of fortified settlements, military encounters, and alliances between different groups highlight the complex web of relationships and power dynamics that shaped the sociopolitical landscape of Cahokia.

13.3 Impact on Society

Warfare and conflicts had profound impacts on Cahokian society. They influenced social hierarchies, political structures, and economic systems. Successful military campaigns and the ability to defend against external threats contributed to the prestige and authority of Cahokian leaders. The control of strategic resources, such as agricultural land, trade routes, and raw materials, played a significant role in the power dynamics within and between communities.

Warfare also had social and cultural implications. It influenced the development of martial ideologies, the commemoration of warriors, and the valorization of bravery and military prowess. Ceremonies and rituals associated with warfare and conflict may have served to unite communities, reinforce social cohesion, and solidify collective identities.

13.4 Complexity and Interpretations

Interpreting warfare in Cahokia is a complex endeavor due to the limited historical records and the inherent biases of archaeological evidence. While fortifications and defensive structures indicate the presence of conflict, they do not provide a complete understanding of the motivations, strategies, and outcomes of warfare. The interpretation of violence and conflict in Cahokia requires a multidisciplinary approach, combining archaeological data, historical accounts, ethnographic analogies, and indigenous perspectives.

Conclusion:

Conflict and warfare were significant aspects of Cahokia's social and political landscape. The presence of fortifications, defensive structures, and historical accounts indicate the existence of intergroup conflicts and territorial disputes. The impact of warfare on Cahokian society influenced power dynamics, social hierarchies, and cultural practices. Understanding the nature of warfare in Cahokia enhances our comprehension of the complex dynamics of pre-Columbian Native American societies and their responses to intergroup conflicts.

Chapter 14: Environmental Context

The ecological setting played a crucial role in shaping the development, resource availability, and sustainability of Cahokia. In this chapter, we will examine the natural environment, climate, and landscape of Cahokia, and explore how these environmental factors influenced settlement patterns, resource utilization, and the long-term viability of the Cahokian civilization.

14.1 Natural Environment

Cahokia was situated in the American Bottom region, an area characterized by its fertile soils, abundant water resources, and diverse ecosystems. The region encompassed a mix of prairies, woodlands, wetlands, and riverine environments, providing a rich array of flora and fauna. The Mississippi River, nearby tributaries, and the surrounding floodplains played a vital role in sustaining the ecosystem, supporting agriculture, and facilitating transportation and trade.

The natural environment of Cahokia offered a range of resources, including fertile agricultural land, timber for construction, clay for pottery production, and a variety of plant and animal species for sustenance and other material needs. The availability of these resources contributed to the growth and prosperity of the Cahokian civilization.

14.2 Climate

The climate of the Cahokia region was characterized by a temperate continental climate, influenced by the proximity of the Mississippi River and the Great Lakes. Summers were generally warm and humid, while winters were cold and occasionally harsh. Seasonal variations in temperature, precipitation, and river levels influenced agricultural practices, resource availability, and settlement patterns.

The cycle of seasonal flooding and receding waters of the Mississippi River played a vital role in Cahokia's agricultural system. Floodwaters enriched the soil, providing fertile conditions for agriculture, while receding waters allowed for the cultivation of crops. The Cahokian people adapted their agricultural practices to the annual flood cycles, capitalizing on the natural rhythms of the environment.

14.3 Settlement Patterns and Resource Utilization

The environmental context influenced settlement patterns and the utilization of resources in Cahokia. The presence of fertile soils and the availability of water resources were key factors in selecting settlement locations. The abundance of arable land in the floodplain allowed for extensive agricultural cultivation, supporting a large population.

Cahokia's settlement pattern was characterized by a central urban core, including the monumental mounds and the central plaza, surrounded by a series of residential and agricultural areas. The proximity to agricultural land ensured a steady supply of food, while access to rivers facilitated trade and transportation.

The diverse ecological setting of Cahokia provided a wide range of resources. The Cahokian people engaged in horticulture, cultivating maize, beans, squash, sunflowers, and other crops. They practiced hunting, fishing, and gathering activities, taking advantage of the rich biodiversity in the region. The woodlands provided timber for construction and fuel, while clay deposits supported pottery production. The Cahokian civilization's ability to sustain itself through a diversified resource base contributed to its resilience and longevity.

14.4 Long-Term Sustainability

The environmental context of Cahokia posed both opportunities and challenges to the long-term sustainability of the civilization. The reliance on agricultural practices, particularly the cultivation of maize, required careful land management, soil conservation, and sustainable agricultural techniques. The Cahokian people implemented strategies such as crop rotation and terracing to mitigate the potential effects of soil depletion and erosion.

However, over time, the increasing population and the demands of an expanding civilization likely put strain on the environment. The intensification of agriculture, deforestation, and the alteration of natural landscapes may have had unintended consequences, such as soil degradation and ecological changes. These factors, combined with potential climatic fluctuations, may have contributed to the eventual decline of Cahokia.

Understanding the environmental context of Cahokia enhances our knowledge of the intricate relationship between human societies and their natural surroundings. It provides insights into the strategies employed by the Cahokian people to adapt to and exploit their environment, as well as the challenges they faced in maintaining long-term sustainability. The study of the environmental context broadens our understanding of the complexities of Cahokia's civilization and its interactions with the natural world.

Chapter 15: Oral Traditions and Cultural Memory

Oral traditions and storytelling played a vital role in preserving and transmitting cultural knowledge in Cahokia. In this chapter, we will explore the significance of oral traditions in the Cahokian context and examine how they contribute to our understanding of Cahokia's history, beliefs, and social practices.

15.1 Importance of Oral Traditions

In the absence of a written language system, the Cahokian people relied on oral traditions as a means of passing down knowledge, history, and cultural values from one generation to another. Through storytelling, songs, chants, and performances, the Cahokian community maintained a rich repository of collective memory, preserving their cultural heritage.

Oral traditions served multiple purposes in Cahokia. They conveyed historical accounts, including narratives about the founding of Cahokia, the lives of important figures, and significant events. They also transmitted spiritual and cosmological beliefs, creation stories, and religious rituals. Additionally, oral traditions played a role in social cohesion, reinforcing shared identities and values within the Cahokian society.

15.2 Oral Traditions and History

Oral traditions provide valuable insights into Cahokia's history. While historical records and archaeological evidence offer glimpses into the past, oral traditions fill gaps and provide alternative perspectives. Stories and legends passed down through generations can shed light on the experiences, struggles, and triumphs of the Cahokian people.

Through oral traditions, we can gain a deeper understanding of the social, political, and economic dynamics of Cahokia. Oral histories may provide details about leadership, political alliances, conflicts, and the daily lives of different social groups. They can offer narratives about trade networks, cultural exchange, and interactions with neighboring communities.

15.3 Spiritual and Cultural Beliefs

Oral traditions were instrumental in preserving and transmitting the spiritual and cultural beliefs of the Cahokian people. Creation stories, myths, and legends explained the origins of the world, the relationships between humans and supernatural beings, and the purpose of religious rituals. These narratives provided a framework for understanding the Cahokian worldview and their place within the cosmos.

The oral traditions associated with religious practices and ceremonies offer valuable insights into Cahokia's spiritual life. They reveal the significance of sacred sites, the roles of religious leaders, and the rituals performed to honor deities or seek divine favor. Understanding these oral traditions enhances our comprehension of Cahokian religious beliefs and the interplay between religion, power, and social cohesion.

15.4 Transmission and Interpretation

The transmission of oral traditions relied on the expertise of designated individuals within the Cahokian society, such as storytellers, shamans, or elders. These individuals possessed the knowledge, skills, and authority to convey the oral narratives accurately. The transmission process often occurred in formal settings, such as communal gatherings, ceremonies, or educational settings.

However, it is important to recognize that oral traditions are not static or fixed. They can evolve, adapt, and incorporate new elements over time. Different storytellers may add their own interpretations or variations, reflecting the evolving social and cultural contexts. As such, oral traditions can provide multiple perspectives and reflect the dynamic nature of Cahokian culture.

15.5 Challenges and Interpretations

Studying oral traditions in the Cahokian context presents certain challenges. Due to the lack of written records and the passage of time, oral traditions may become fragmented or subject to memory distortion. Researchers must approach oral narratives with caution, employing critical analysis and considering multiple sources of information to corroborate and contextualize the oral accounts.

Interpreting oral traditions requires a collaborative approach, engaging with indigenous communities, scholars, and descendants of the Cahokian people. Indigenous perspectives and traditional knowledge can provide valuable insights into the meaning, symbolism, and cultural nuances embedded within oral narratives.

Conclusion:

Oral traditions and storytelling played a pivotal role in preserving and transmitting cultural knowledge in Cahokia. They served as a medium for conveying history, spiritual beliefs, and social practices. Understanding and interpreting oral traditions allow us to access the rich cultural heritage of Cahokia, providing a more comprehensive understanding of this vibrant pre-Columbian civilization.

Chapter 16: Comparative Perspectives

In this chapter, we will undertake a comparative analysis of Cahokia with other ancient civilizations from around the world. By examining similarities, differences, and broader implications, we can gain a deeper understanding of urbanism and complex societies in different cultural contexts.

16.1 Urbanism and City Planning

Cahokia's status as a pre-Columbian urban center invites comparison with other ancient cities such as Teotihuacan, Rome, and Angkor. Through comparative analysis, we can explore commonalities and variations in urban planning, architecture, and social organization.

By examining the layout, infrastructure, and architectural features of Cahokia, we can identify parallels with other ancient cities. Comparative analysis may reveal shared principles of urban design, such as the centralization of power, hierarchical spatial organization, and the construction of monumental structures as symbols of authority.

16.2 Sociopolitical Organization

Comparative analysis allows us to explore the sociopolitical organization of Cahokia in relation to other ancient civilizations. Examining the roles of ruling elites, the existence of social hierarchies, and mechanisms of governance provides a broader understanding of power dynamics and social complexity.

Comparisons with civilizations like the Maya, Inca, or ancient Egypt can shed light on the extent of Cahokia's centralization of power, administrative structures, and social stratification. Understanding similarities and differences in sociopolitical organization contributes to a more nuanced comprehension of ancient societies and the factors influencing their development.

16.3 Economic Systems and Trade Networks

Comparative analysis of economic systems and trade networks helps us situate Cahokia within a broader global context. By examining similarities and differences in trade routes, goods exchanged, and economic practices, we can gain insights into the complexities of interregional and long-distance trade.

Comparisons with civilizations like the Silk Road networks, the Hanseatic League, or the maritime trade of the Indian Ocean highlight the interconnectedness of ancient societies and the importance of trade for urban development. Understanding the scale and scope of Cahokia's trade networks enhances our understanding of its economic prosperity and regional influence.

16.4 Cultural Expressions and Artistic Traditions

Comparative analysis of artistic expressions and cultural traditions broadens our perspective on the diversity of ancient civilizations. By exploring similarities and differences in art, architecture, and symbolic representations, we can discern unique cultural identities and shared artistic motifs.

Comparisons with civilizations like the Maya, Ancient Greece, or ancient China elucidate the distinctiveness of Cahokian artistic traditions. Identifying common themes or influences across different cultures enhances our appreciation of the interplay between art, culture, and societal values.

16.5 Lessons and Implications

By undertaking comparative analysis, we can draw lessons and implications for the study of urbanism and complex societies. Understanding the similarities and differences between Cahokia and other ancient civilizations expands our knowledge of the factors that contribute to the rise, flourishing, and decline of complex societies throughout history.

Comparative perspectives encourage interdisciplinary approaches, facilitating the exchange of knowledge and methodologies between scholars studying different civilizations. This cross-pollination of ideas enriches our understanding of human history, urban development, and societal dynamics.

Furthermore, comparative analysis invites us to question assumptions and biases inherent in the study of ancient civilizations. It prompts us to consider the role of cultural context, environmental factors, and local circumstances in shaping diverse expressions of urbanism and societal complexity.

Conclusion:

Comparative analysis provides a valuable framework for understanding Cahokia within a global context. By examining similarities, differences, and broader implications, we gain a more comprehensive understanding of urbanism, complex societies, and the intricacies of human civilization throughout time.

Chapter Conclusion

In this book, we have explored various aspects of Cahokia, shedding light on its significance and contributions to Native American history and archaeology.

Let us now summarize the key points discussed in each chapter.

Chapter 1: The Mississippian Culture

- Overview of the Mississippian culture and its characteristics

- Cultural practices, social organization, and religious beliefs of the Mississippian people

- Connection between Cahokia and the broader Mississippian culture

Chapter 2: The City of Cahokia

- Location, geography, and natural resources of Cahokia

- Layout and architecture of the city, including the mounds and the central plaza

- Population estimates and daily life in Cahokia

Chapter 3: Trade and Economy

- Importance of trade networks and commerce in Cahokia's prosperity

- Description of trade routes, goods exchanged, and economic activities

- Role of Cahokia as a regional trade hub and its connections to other Native American societies

Chapter 4: Social and Political Structure

- Hierarchical social structure and class divisions in Cahokia

- Roles and responsibilities of the ruling elite and commoners

- Political organization and governance in Cahokia

Chapter 5: Religion and Ceremonial Life

- Spiritual beliefs and religious practices of the Cahokian people

- Description of the major religious sites and rituals

- Relationship between religion, power, and social cohesion in Cahokia

Chapter 6: Decline and Legacy

- Theories and debates surrounding the decline of Cahokia

- Possible factors contributing to the city's decline, such as environmental changes and sociopolitical unrest

- Influence and legacy of Cahokia on later Native American cultures and modern society

Chapter 7: Excavations and Preservation

- Overview of archaeological excavations and discoveries at Cahokia

- Discussion of the preservation efforts and the establishment of Cahokia Mounds State Historic Site

- Importance of ongoing research and future prospects for understanding Cahokia

Chapter 8: Art and Symbolism

- Exploration of the artistic expressions and symbolism in Cahokia, including pottery, sculptures, and rock art

- Analysis of the meaning and cultural significance of these artistic creations, providing insights into Cahokia's aesthetics and belief systems

Chapter 9: Astronomy and Cosmology

- Investigation of Cahokia's understanding and observation of celestial phenomena

- Examination of astronomical alignments, structures, and rituals that reflect the Cahokian people's relationship with the cosmos

Chapter 10: Agriculture and Foodways

- In-depth exploration of Cahokia's agricultural practices, including crop cultivation, land management, and food production

- Examination of the significance of agriculture in sustaining the city's population and supporting its growth

Chapter 11: Gender and Society

- Analysis of gender roles, relationships, and power dynamics in Cahokia society

- Exploration of the roles of women and men in different spheres of life, including economic activities, religious practices, and political structures

Chapter 12: Conflict and Warfare

- Investigation of warfare practices, intergroup conflicts, and territorial disputes in the Cahokian context

- Analysis of archaeological evidence and historical accounts shedding light on the nature of warfare in Cahokia and its impact on the society

Chapter 13: Environmental Context

- Examination of the ecological setting of Cahokia, including the natural environment, climate, and landscape

- Discussion of how environmental factors influenced settlement patterns, resource availability, and the long-term sustainability of Cahokia

Chapter 14: Oral Traditions and Cultural Memory

- Exploration of the role of oral traditions and storytelling in preserving and transmitting cultural knowledge in Cahokia

- Examination of how oral traditions contribute to our understanding of Cahokia's history, beliefs, and social practices

Chapter 15: Comparative Perspectives

- Comparative analysis of Cahokia with other ancient civilizations around the world, exploring similarities, differences, and broader implications for the study of urbanism and complex societies

Through this comprehensive exploration, we have come to appreciate the multifaceted nature of Cahokia. Its significance in North American history, the complexity of its social, political, and religious systems, and its influence on later Native American cultures and modern society are evident.

Cahokia continues to be an area of active research and discovery. Ongoing excavations, preservation efforts, and interdisciplinary studies contribute to our evolving understanding of this remarkable ancient city.

By delving into additional chapters, we have also touched upon other intriguing aspects of Cahokia, such as its artistic expressions, astronomy and cosmology, agriculture and foodways, gender dynamics, conflict and warfare, environmental context, and the role of oral traditions. These chapters further enrich our comprehension of Cahokia and its place in the broader tapestry of human history.

As we conclude this book, it is important to recognize that Cahokia stands as a testament to the complexity, achievements, and resilience of pre-Columbian Native American civilizations. Exploring its history not only deepens our understanding of the past but also fosters a greater appreciation for the rich and diverse cultural heritage of the Americas.

Chapter: References and Additional Resources

For readers who wish to further explore the history, culture, and significance of Cahokia, this chapter provides a curated list of recommended resources, including books, articles, websites, and museums. These resources offer valuable insights and opportunities for deeper engagement with the subject matter.

1. Books:

- "Cahokia: Ancient America's Great City on the Mississippi" by Timothy R. Pauketat: This book provides a comprehensive overview of Cahokia, covering its history, archaeology, and cultural significance. Pauketat's engaging narrative explores the rise and decline of Cahokia and its connections to broader Native American civilizations.

- "Cahokia Mounds: America's First City" edited by Bill Iseminger: This anthology features contributions from leading archaeologists and scholars, offering diverse perspectives on Cahokia's history, cultural practices, and its impact on Native American archaeology.

- "The Cahokia Atlas: A Historical Atlas of Cahokia Archaeology" by Melvin Fowler and Tamira Brennan: This atlas presents detailed maps, illustrations, and archaeological data, providing a visual exploration of Cahokia's landscape, architecture, and archaeological features.

2. Articles and Academic Papers:

- "The Archaeology of Cahokia" by Thomas E. Emerson and R. Barry Lewis: This article provides a comprehensive overview of the archaeological research conducted at Cahokia, discussing key discoveries, interpretive challenges, and future research directions.

- "Cahokia and the Archaeology of Power" by Susan M. Alt, Timothy R. Pauketat, and Thomas E. Emerson: This scholarly article explores the complex social and political structures of Cahokia, shedding light on power dynamics and social organization within the ancient city.

3. Websites:

- Cahokia Mounds State Historic Site (cahokiamounds.org): The official website of Cahokia Mounds State Historic Site offers a wealth of information about the ancient city, including visitor information, educational resources, and updates on ongoing research and preservation efforts.

- Illinois State Archaeological Survey (isas.illinois.edu): The Illinois State Archaeological Survey website provides access to various research publications, reports, and archaeological resources related to Cahokia and the broader Illinois region.

4. Museums and Archaeological Sites:

- Cahokia Mounds State Historic Site, Illinois, USA: A visit to Cahokia Mounds State Historic Site allows you to explore the archaeological remains of Cahokia, including the mounds, interpretive centers, and exhibits that showcase the history and culture of the Cahokian people.

- The National Museum of the American Indian, Washington, D.C., USA: This museum features exhibitions dedicated to the indigenous cultures of the Americas, including exhibits that touch upon the history and legacy of Cahokia and other Native American civilizations.

- The Field Museum, Chicago, Illinois, USA: The Field Museum houses a significant collection of artifacts from Cahokia and other archaeological sites, providing insights into the material culture and daily life of the Cahokian people.

These resources serve as a starting point for further exploration and research on Cahokia. They offer a range of perspectives, from scholarly analyses to accessible introductions, allowing readers to deepen their understanding of Cahokia's significance in Native American history and archaeology.